Mission-shaped Church

Missionary Values, Church Planting and Fresh Expressions of Church

Paul Bayes

National Mission and Evangelism Adviser
Mission and Public Affairs Division, Archbishops' Council

GROVE BOOKS LIMITED
RIDLEY HALL RD CAMBRIDGE CB3 9HU

Contents

The Cover Illustration is by Peter Ashton

First Impression August 2004
ISSN 1367-0840
ISBN 1 85174 569 6

Introduction

He said, 'You don't build a house by starting with the roof and working down. You start with the foundations.' They said, 'What does that
mean?' He said, 'The foundation is our neighbour whom we must
win. The neighbour is where we start. Every commandment of Christ
depends on this.'[1]

Mission-shaped Church could be one of the most important reports the Church
of England has produced for decades. Or it could be yet another book for the
dusty top shelf. Which of those it is depends on how the Church reads it, and
what we will do to follow it up.

This matters very much to me. I am working for the Archbishops' Council as
national mission and evangelism adviser, encouraging the Church to follow
up the report and especially its recommendations. I came into post in Janu-
ary 2004, two weeks before *Mission-shaped Church* was published, and the
report is the reason I applied for the job.

For over 20 years I have been a local church leader who has tried to listen out
for what God has been saying and doing in my own context, and to plant
and grow church accordingly. Ten years ago I read *Breaking New Ground* and
was inspired by that report to think as creatively as I could about new ways
of being church in this culture. More recently I was involved in a parallel cell
church/team ministry on the edge of Southampton.[2]

I was not involved in the writing of *Mission-shaped Church*. But I believe that
in God's economy it has come to the Church of England at a time of huge
opportunity and potential. The report will be a key part of the growth and
renewal of the church in our time, as long as we use it as a tool for laying a
foundation and not as a decorative flagpole.

Building on Values

This booklet is not a précis of *Mission-shaped Church*. The report itself is co-
herent, clear, short and a best-seller.[3] What I want to do here is to encourage
a particular way of reading and implementing *Mission-shaped Church*—a way
that I am calling values-based, and not bandwagon-driven. I will be looking
at the report's 'missionary values' in the hope that they can be seen as the
foundation for a church shaped for mission.

Mission-shaped Church is story-rich and contains a great many detailed and interesting examples. But these are not meant to be a lucky bag of bright ideas which can be imported into an ailing situation in order to make everything all right there. What the report offers instead is much more valuable—a theological base, and a set of values.

Values and Bandwagons

They asked the bishop, 'Will the church planters get to heaven?' 'Yes,' he replied, 'as long as they don't run past the door.'[4]

Lots of church leaders care deeply about mission. This deep concern motivates people, but it can also make them worried. When we look to the future of the church we have to be honest and say that there is a lot of anxiety around at the moment. The graphs are not looking good, and the respectful hearing we used to assume from the world has been lost. The mission field often seems stony and unproductive. Our work does not match the need. We seem to be in the business of tending window boxes when we should be farming.

Why? We still believe the gospel, and we believe in the power of God through the preaching of the gospel to grow the fruit of the Spirit and transform the world. But somehow the way we are shaping the church is not bringing that fruit in the way we so much want to see.

This makes for anxiety; anxiety gives birth to haste. What will solve our problems *now*?

This nervous haste hovers around in the air, gathering force like an electrical charge, and when the church hears that something seems to be working somewhere, the anxiety and haste earth to it and we see the lightning and hear the thunder. Another bandwagon has been created. So we leap aboard, and it rolls along, wildly and excitingly, for a couple of hundred yards. But then for some reason the wheels begin to wobble, and then they fall off, and everyone gets tired, and the cry goes up, 'we tried that, and it didn't work!'—and we get anxious and start looking around again.

I am an example of what I mean. As an anxious vicar I carry the scars of a great many conferences, and the ruptures of a man who has tried to lift his church on to a great many bandwagons.

And so in my case, when the rumours of cell church came along, nine or ten years ago, my anxiety earthed to that as well. Maybe this was the thing that would make everything all right! When could we start?

Even as I felt this anxious urge I knew that it was mistaken. God's will for the church could not be so frantic. So when I went to hear Bill Beckham speak at a cell church training seminar in the mid–90s, it came as such a relief to hear him say, echoing Ralph Neighbour, 'We don't think you should change a single structure in your church until you've established the right values in your church.'[5]

Classical cell-church teaching, like the teaching of the Willow Creek Community Church and any other teaching that comes out of a genuinely mission-shaped church, insists that listening prayer comes first and values follow, before you build a thing. If bandwagons come instead, it is because people have not been listening.

For me this was a real liberation, a deliverance from the tyranny of the anxious. And it is also the spirit of this report. I believe that it is here—in the realm of the church's foundations—that the real work of *Mission-shaped Church* begins.

A Moment of Opportunity 2

The point that Bishop Graham made, that seemed to me absolutely crucial for this Synod to grasp, is that we stand at something of a *kairos* moment. A number of things are coming together...[6]

In God every moment is a moment of opportunity. Even so, it is possible, as Rowan Williams did in this speech to General Synod, to spot the movement of the Spirit of God from time to time and to identify a focusing, a 'thickening of the plot,' that paves the way for the *kairos* moment, God's special moment.

A number of things have indeed been coming together, not only in the lead-up to that Synod debate but over a number of years. Steadily, church-planting and church-shaping has been moving from the edge of the church's concern to its heart.

Oddballs

15 years ago those of us who spoke warmly of church planting were viewed across a rather glum spectrum, from bewildered indifference to gentle suspicion (and sometimes not so gentle). To many Church of England people

we were an odd bunch who were looking the wrong way. Perhaps we were looking to the Church Growth movement ('Very *American*, you know, Paul'), or maybe to the wilder shores of mid-west Protestantism and redneck Pentecostalism, or possibly again to some odd distortion of the gospel from the two-thirds world. Wherever we were looking it was the wrong way, and people thought we were abandoning our Anglican roots for something that glittered but was not gold.

Nonetheless church planting had caught on. Bob and Mary Hopkins of Anglican Church Planting Initiatives had begun their tireless work of researching and teaching. George Lings and others had begun to gather data, make sense of it, and share it. Numbers rose—to 370 plants in the years from 1978 to the present, with 90% still in being today. And in 1991, four of these were planted without obtaining the necessary permissions. Both the catching-on and the law-breaking caused the church to think.

Hope and Fear—Breaking New Ground [7]

Ten years ago, with the publishing of *Breaking New Ground*, the official Church unfolded some of its thinking about what church planting, this worldwide ferment, might have to say to us. That thinking was driven by two impulses—hope and fear. The first two paragraphs of *Breaking New Ground* show this clearly:

> 1.1 When a congregation looks outward in mission, and considers strategies for evangelism, it may be that some of the most exciting possibilities for that parish involve planting a new church...
>
> 1.2 Those instances where such a strategy has involved crossing the established boundary of a parish or diocese have now thrown a spotlight onto the whole concept and practice of church planting...

In the words of its first chapter-heading, was church planting 'opportunity or danger'? In the end *Breaking New Ground* thought it was both. Church planting had something very good to offer provided there was goodwill on all sides when things began. But sometimes there was not goodwill. Then we had to be careful—very careful. 'Diversity feels safer if we know that it will be contained within certain areas and will not "stray"'(p 1).

Glimpsing the Network Society

> An understanding of evangelization that embraces the whole of our individual and corporate life has to move in a direction that takes seriously the neighbourhoods and networks in which we live.
>
> *(Breaking New Ground, p 4)*

Meanwhile the context—the post-industrial western world—continued to change, and with bewildering speed. *Breaking New Ground* was one of the first Anglican documents to grapple positively with the impact of postmodernity. It began to recognize the challenge and the opportunity of network culture—'…it is possible to see that it is networks which are now the communities to which we feel a predominant loyalty' (p 3).

The report began to get to grips with what that meant for the parish system and for the way we might do church. It was a cautious report, but *Breaking New Ground* pointed accurately to a changing context, and it helped to create and foster an atmosphere of experiment and release, of permission-giving.

The Decade of Evangelism

Breaking New Ground was published in 1994, as the Decade of Evangelism was building its momentum.

The Decade has often received a bad press. Many were happy at its end to point to statistics showing numerical decline throughout it. Yet like all godly initiatives, the Decade was values-driven, too, and was never meant to be a bandwagon.[8] Essentially it was a season of laying foundations, of research, of questioning and listening and prayer; above all a season devoted to re-setting the compass of the Church. There are no quick fixes in God's economy, and all those who were prepared to use the Decade as a focus for their Christian obedience understood that.

It is through that spirit of patient attention that the Decade blessed (and still blesses) the shape of the church. A developing theology of mission brought new ways of being church to centre stage. The ongoing work of evangelism came to be seen as the work of the community, not simply something to be delegated to gifted individuals and then forgotten by the rest. People re-read Ephesians 4 with its emphasis on the equipping of the saints and saw that the evangelists were called to equip the saints for the work of that ministry, too. Robert Warren began to focus his teaching about the missionary shape of the congregation.[9] Lesslie Newbigin spoke of the hermeneutic of the gospel being a community that lived and proclaimed its reality.[10] So we were encouraged to be creative in exploring what a church would look like if it were shaped for mission and really making disciples of its people.

Many Currents, One Stream

Other Christian denominations and groupings are walking this road with, and often ahead of, the Anglican family. In the Baptist world church planting has come to be seen as a clear path for ministers-in-training, and for years now Spurgeon's College has offered a church planting track as well as its pastoral training. Anglican covenant partners from the Methodist Church were represented on the *Mission-shaped Church* working party and contributed a good deal of experience to its thinking. The new churches, which have pioneered a good many of these things in England, are increasingly open to dialogue and partnership in local situations across the country. Roman Catholic Base Ecclesial Communities, in the two-thirds world and in Europe, continue to stimulate and inspire small-group church pioneers here. Similarly, the Roman Catholic new religious communities (such as Focolare, Chemin Neuf and the Sion Community for Evangelization) are a rich resource through which God has much to teach us all, particularly as much of it comes from the aggressively secular context of urban mainland Europe. Many of these new community movements are responding directly to a network society, and they spread with the blessing and encouragement of the Pope and of local Roman Catholic hierarchies. Almost all of them have an ecumenical dimension.

Fresh Expressions and Anglican roots

Anglicans can take their place naturally among all this. They belong to a Christian family that finds its roots and its validation in building an appropriate mission-shaped church. The phrase 'fresh expressions of church,' with its conscious reflection of the Declaration of Assent, points to that focus on mission that has always been at the heart of our tradition.[11]

It is worth recalling the opening words of that Declaration of Assent, put to all clergy at ordination and to clergy, Lay Workers and Readers whenever they are licensed to new work. It is a vibrant affirmation both of faith and of purpose. It combines great confidence and clarity in the heart of the Christian gospel with an explicit call to openness and flexibility in its expression. It need not be dusty and legal. Let us give it a clean-up. Why not look at it this way—almost as a poem? (see grey box)

> The Church of England is part
> of the One,
> Holy, Catholic
> and Apostolic Church,
> worshipping the one
> true God,
> Father, Son and Holy Spirit.
> It professes the faith
> uniquely
> revealed in the Holy Scriptures
> and set forth in the catholic creeds,
> which faith the Church is called upon
> to proclaim
> **afresh**
> in each generation...[12]

Imagination and the Mixed Economy

3

Imagination and the Archbishop

> I hope with all my heart that I can serve to nurture confidence and conviction in our Church, and to help Christian faith to capture the imagination of our people and our culture.[13]

Imagination and re-imagination is the ground and theme of all that Rowan Williams has been seeking to do since his appointment as Archbishop of Canterbury. This single appointment has done a great deal to foster the acceptance of emerging-church thinking across the Church of England.

Rowan Williams has 'form' as a church-planting bishop. As long ago as 1993, as Bishop of Monmouth, he blessed and encouraged the planting and building of 'Living Proof,' a community project that issued in a new way of being church, whose story formed the first of George Lings' *Encounters on the Edge* booklets.[14]

It is this Archbishop who, supported by the Lambeth Trustees and the Lambeth Partners, has established 'Fresh Expressions,' the successor to 'Springboard,' to be led by Steven Croft. This initiative will play an absolutely vital and creative part in the development of *Mission-shaped Church* thinking across the Church of England. It will be well resourced and will operate in the creative space between the institutional church and the mission agencies.

It is this Archbishop who said to the General Synod in York in 2003:

> Mission, it's been said, is finding out what God is doing and joining in. And at present there is actually an extraordinary amount going on in terms of the creation of new styles of church life. We can call it church planting, 'new ways of being church' or various other things; but the point is that more and more patterns of worship and shared life are appearing on the edge of our mainstream life that cry out for our support, understanding and nurture if they are not to get isolated and unaccountable...All of these are church in the sense that they are what happens when the invitation of Jesus is received and people recognize it in each other.
>
> Can we live with this and make it work?[15]

It seems clear that a culture of permission-giving is Archbishop Rowan's intention. He has compared the situation of church leaders at present to that of the medieval pope Innocent III, 'the patron saint of permission-givers,' who was approached out of the blue by Francis of Assisi with his plans for the renewal of the church.[16] Surprisingly (prompted it is said by a vision from the Lord) Innocent III released the oddball friar to go out and preach and to establish a new form of Christian community, with enormously fruitful results.

The Mixed Economy: Mix, Not Fudge

> Well, then, I suspect, it's a lot more chaotic than we have usually assumed. We used to, in Wales, talk about the 'mixed economy' church—that is, one which is learning how to cope with diverse forms and rhythms of worshipping life. Tearing up the rule book and trying to replace the parochial system is a recipe for disaster and wasted energy. In all kinds of places, the parochial system is working remarkably. It's just that we are increasingly aware of the contexts where it simply isn't capable of making an impact, where something has to grow out of it or alongside it, not as a rival (why do we cast so much of our Christian life in terms of competition?) but as an attempt to answer questions that the parish system was never meant to answer.[17]

Mission-shaped Church is radical. *Breaking New Ground* saw church planting and fresh expressions of church as a 'supplement' to the main point of Anglican life, the sustaining of the parish system. This 'supplementary' vision can give the impression that the emerging church is designed, like dietary supplements, to be a necessary but rather unpalatable addition to an otherwise tasty meal.[18]

Then in Wales in 1999 Rowan Williams began to talk about the 'mixed economy' of old and new in the Anglican family. This phrase came with him to Canterbury and came into our vocabulary more widely. As this happened, *Mission-shaped Church* arrived on the Anglican scene.

The mixed economy is not an Anglican fudge. We are not speaking about wanting a church that mixes up mission shapes and anti-mission shapes. Mixed-economy thinking assumes that all church should be shaped for mission. And yet what a given church actually looks like—whether it is a community in an ancient building or a community on a cyber-network, whether it is alt.worship or bcp.matins—what it looks like is absolutely beside the point. The point is, is that shape the shape for mission in that context? The answer will be found in that church's foundational values.

Missionary Values

4

First Things First

Values take their place between an awareness and understanding of who and how God is, and the structures and shapes that Christians build to serve God. They are the vital building block that prevents anxious haste from collapsing our hopes. This diagram sketches the way to go—and where you begin your journey on this circle is all-important.

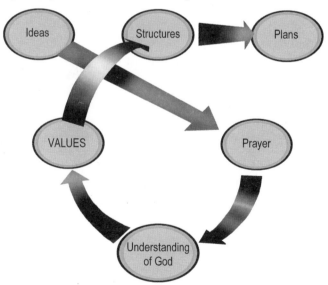

Change flows from our prayer, leading to a deeper awareness and understanding of who God is—then to our values—and only then to changing structures and making plans.

So theology and prayer come first. *Mission-shaped Church* clearly stresses that the credal foundation of the church, the faith which needs to be 'proclaimed afresh,' is not itself a value of the church. The church flows from the gospel of God. 'It's not the church of God that has a mission, but the God of mission who has a church.'[20]

Five Marks of Mission

The values of *Mission-shaped Church* were not written in a vacuum. They echo and sharpen the mission values of the Anglican Communion as a whole.

These are caught in the 'five marks of mission' of the Anglican Consultative Council, adopted in 1988 at the Lambeth Conference and in 1994 by the General Synod, and affirmed in *Mission-shaped Church*:

- To proclaim the good news of the kingdom;
- To teach, baptize and nurture new believers;
- To respond to human need by loving service;
- To seek to transform unjust structures of society;
- To strive to safeguard the integrity of creation and sustain and renew the earth.[21]

Reviewing these more recently, the ACC said:

The first mark of mission…is really a summary of what *all* mission is about, because it is based on Jesus' own summary of his mission (Matthew 4.17, Mark 1.14–15, Luke 4.18, Luke 7.22; *cf* John 3.14–17). Instead of being just one (albeit the first) of five distinct activities, this should be the key statement about *everything* we do in mission.

Five Values for a Missionary Church

Building on this, *Mission-shaped Church* identifies its five values for a missionary church.[22]

- **A missionary church is focused on God the Trinity**
  Worship lies at the heart of a missionary church, and to love and know God as Father, Son and Spirit is its chief inspiration and primary purpose…

- **A missionary church is incarnational**
  It seeks to shape itself in relation to the culture in which it is located or to which it is called…

- **A missionary church is transformational**
  It exists for the transformation of the community that it serves, through the power of the gospel and the Holy Spirit...

- **A missionary church makes disciples**
  It is active in calling people to faith in Jesus Christ... It encourages the gifting and vocation of all the people of God, and invests in the development of leaders. It is concerned for the transformation of individuals, as well as for the transformation of communities.

- **A missionary church is relational**
  ...It is characterized by welcome and hospitality. Its ethos and style are open to change when new members join.

5

Grounded in the Trinity: The Hinge-Value

Abbot Pastor said, 'People must breathe humility and the fear of God just as ceaselessly as they inhale and exhale the air.'[23]

Don't Be Afraid[24]

The first missionary value is the hinge between our understanding of God and the other values that flow from this. In much of his writing in the Decade of Evangelism Robert Warren was concerned to place spirituality at the heart of our thinking about church: 'The state of this "heart" is the crucial factor in the effectiveness of any local church.'[25]

In the end what will free the church from anxiety? In the words of our Lord, 'This kind can come out only through prayer'(Mark 9.29).

We need to be very clear about this. For those whose minds are so inclined, planning, analysis and strategizing can be great fun, sometimes even addictively so. The risk with moving too quickly to this is that we come to think of God as a poor old soul who cannot really get his act together unless we give him a little training.

Much of *Mission-shaped Church* builds on the self-emptying of Jesus Christ, following Philippians 2, on his total immersion in the world, even to the cross. This is the incarnational value, central to any understanding of the Christian mission. But in its list of values the report has not put this first.

We do not act as regents for an absent king

For *Mission-shaped Church* the *primary* missionary value is that we look to God as God is, to the life of the Trinity. We do not act as regents for an absent king. We practice his presence, sharing in God's mission first and last. Absorbing the truth of this leads to a trusting dependence, and cures anxiety, by emphasizing the glory and the transcendence of God. It puts all our missionary endeavour in the widest perspective.

Incarnation and Cross: Dying to Live

6

The first value leads us to trust in a God who is on the case both now and to the end of time, and to build a spirituality.

Then the incarnational value leads to a principle and a method—that of double listening: listening to God and listening to the cultural context.[26] A church that listens both ways will be culturally relevant, but also counter-cultural in its obedience to the gospel. And as it has always been, this is costly.

'And being found in human form, he humbled himself and became obedient to the point of death—even death on a cross' (Phil 2.7, 8). It is not possible to set out on the road of incarnation without encountering the cross. In the end a church shaped for mission is one shaped to meet its cultural context, and therefore by definition *not* a church shaped to suit the preferences of its own members.

Spirit and Flesh

In Romans 8.6ff St Paul famously distinguished between the flesh and the Spirit. The distinction is familiar, and we know that Paul is not opposing the created world (the flesh) with some ethereal realm (spirit). Instead he is looking at the whole of life—corporeal, structural, mental, spiritual—and asks: 'Is that whole facing God (spirit) or is it turned away from him (flesh)?' As we reflect on the incarnational value, this way of looking at things bears examination in the context of our ways of doing church.

'People look on outward appearance, but God looks on the heart' (1 Sam 16.7). So perhaps you could imagine a church community that has started a BCP Communion for frightened and lonely old people in a residential home, a liturgy that the church people themselves do not find particularly fruitful in their own prayers, but which they offer in order to lead the residents closer to their Lord through a once-deserted, half-remembered liturgy. That community builds a place of worship and of friendship in that home—church according to the Spirit, mission-shaped church.

And perhaps you could imagine a handful of exhausted charismatics in a school hall, gathered round their OHP (because data projectors are a bit newfangled), singing the songs of the 80s, still trying to keep their church plant on the road, not knowing why no one seems interested any more in something that meant so much to them when it began. Worried about the worship group, how to keep it all going, wishing there was a Royal College of Bass Guitarists who could help. Determined above all not to change the thing they love so much. And, heroic and courageous as it might be, in the end that would be church according to the flesh.

Dying to Live

Obedient immersion in the culture is costly, even to the death of the church we love. An early draft of the report was called 'Dying to live.' Aware of what the media might make of such a title ('Church admits it's dying,' and so on), the final report bears another name. But it cannot be stressed enough that it is the principle of dying to live that is at the heart of *Mission-shaped Church*. Double listening involves an asceticism, a discipline of the heart.

For those called to plant churches, and to express church afresh, this discipline can be painful. Most of us come to faith within a tradition that becomes precious to us. The task of seeing what it is in that tradition that is eternal, and what it is that is our own cultural baggage, is never an easy one. It is particularly hard for people who have come to faith through a style of doing church that is 'modern,' 'informal,' 'unchurchy,' because human traditions are very quick-setting cement indeed.

When I introduced small-group life to one of the churches I led in the 80s, the concept of worshipping together in a front room was quite new to us all. So we played some Vineyard tapes, listening to the worship and worshipping along. After three weeks I suggested that the groups might like to sing songs to God with their own voices. 'But' came the response, indignant and hurt, 'but we *always* play tapes!'

Cloning, Anxiety and Preference

One in ten of the Church of England's church plants has failed, the major reason being that they were not plants but clones. They bore insufficient resemblance to the receiving community and they never took root.[27]

The incarnational value, dying to live, cuts the root of cloning the church.

Mission-shaped Church is clear that cloning does not work. The temptation to clone is rooted in anxiety. Pioneer church planters tend to be, and usually need to be, people with entrepreneurial and often extravert gifts. Living with ambiguity and uncertainty is particularly unsettling for them. And the fact is that much of what falls under the star of *Mission-shaped Church* will be provisional and fragile, with the jury out on its long-term viability for a long time, maybe for some years.

In such an atmosphere the temptation to clone a successful model is very strong. The first two values will combat that temptation. Trusting God in the face of apparent failure gives heart. The discipline of listening, of journeying out to others and being changed by them, gives direction to the courage of a mission-shaped people.[28]

The touchstone of whether the incarnational value has been lived is *surprise*. Is the community where a church has been planted surprised by what has appeared—but equally is the planting community itself surprised by what God has formed in their midst?

Hunger, and a Surprise

Mission-shaped Church tells the story of a Plymouth parish using a model of listening drawn from Latin American Base Ecclesial Communities:

> The intention here was not to copy Latin American models, but to adapt them to context using common tools and processes. The churches asked the questions 'What is the Lord saying to us? What does he want us to do? What use is the church in this community and what difference is it making?'...One result was that a small sailing yacht, donated to a Plymouth parish, evolved into a staffed programme with a fleet of boats, enriching the lives of disadvantaged young people in the city.[29]

A fleet in Plymouth—it sounds highly culturally appropriate. Yet it began, not as a good idea, but as a spiritual question, 'What is the Lord saying to us?'

The answer to that question may not come quickly. The question may be the precursor to months of uncertainly and muddle—which is what double listening can feel like. The temptation is always there to find a quick fix, maybe to open *Mission-shaped Church* and stick a pin into it to find a good example to copy, a decent bandwagon to leap aboard. But God's economy is different:

> Remember the long way the Lord your God has led you these forty years in the wilderness, in order to humble you, testing you to know what was in your heart, whether or not you would keep his commandment. He humbled you by letting you hunger, then by feeding you with manna, with which neither you nor your ancestors were acquainted...
> (Deuteronomy 8.2, 3a)

> And the Spirit immediately drove him out into the wilderness...and he was with the wild beasts; and the angels waited on him. (Mk 1.12, 13)

Hunger, then new food which comes as a great surprise. Is not that the dynamic of a mission-shaped church?

7 Transformational Church: Making All Things New

Whole-loaf, whole-life Christianity embraces the wonders and griefs of humanity in all its fullness in God's world.[30]

A missionary church exists for the transformation of the community that it serves, through the power of the gospel and the Holy Spirit. It is not self-serving, self-seeking or self-focused. The kingdom of God is its goal, and church is understood as a servant and sign of God's kingdom in its community, whether neighbourhood or network.[31]

'Parochial' has become a dirty word. It implies an inward-looking or backward-looking provincial attitude. Its root is the word 'parish,' which has always meant a lot to Anglicans, but which has got a bit dirty too—and not without reason. For a good many Christians 'our parish' has come to mean 'our neighbourhood' and also, too often, 'our defended territory.' Within the Church of England, creative and hopeful initiatives have shipwrecked on the grumpy insistence of parishes that only they can decide what God should be doing 'on their patch.'

We are placed where we are by God for the sake of the world, not of our own brand of church

Mission-shaped Church is very clear that God's people are called to leave this sort of parochial thinking far behind. Those who are locked into this defensiveness need to grow up before they grow old. Not only the coming of a network society, but the coming of Christian courage and love, should consign such fortress-church thinking to the dustbin.

But 'parish' means, or could mean, a good deal more than this dour picture of defensive foolishness. 'Parish' speaks, or could speak, of God's love for the world. The traditional understanding of the Church of England is that we are placed where we are by God for the sake of the world, not of our own brand of church. In such an understanding 'parish' means all the life of a given place, of a given culture. Alan Ecclestone wrote movingly about this wide and intense calling of the Church in his book *A Staircase for Silence*.[32] *Mission-shaped Church* is calling the Christian community to be immersed in the 'parish' and to watch and work with God for transformation there.

This vision of 'parish' is not threatened by the shift to a network society. In his speech replying to the debate on *Mission-shaped Church* in the General Synod, Bishop James Jones said:

> In Anglican missiology there is an unbroken thread from pastoral care to evangelism, but in the 21st century people live not only in parishes; they also inhabit what I call 'invisible parishes,' relationships that transcend geographical boundaries through work, leisure, common interests.[33]

It is to this sense of parish, visible and invisible, that *Mission-shaped Church* points through its transformation value. Network-flows have indeed taken first place in our lives—substantially so if we are urban people, increasingly so if we are rural people.[34]

However, the report is not saying that the role of the church is to establish a few Christian networks, parallel to those in the culture, and to channel believers out of other networks and into these, in a postmodern version of John Stott's famous 'Christian rabbit-holes':

> In the morning they *(the Christian rabbits)* pop out of their safe Christian homes, hold their breath at work, scurry home to their families and then off to their Bible studies, and finally end the day praying for the unbelievers they safely avoided all day.[35]

If the networks are 'invisible parish' then the transformation value calls the church to serve the kingdom by transforming those networks by means of the good news of Jesus Christ for them, and in the power of the Spirit of God. Out of this work of transformation, new ways of being church emerge— and 'the church is a community that demonstrates this decisive transformation as really experienceable.'[36]

Inculturation is the necessary call of the God of mission to his church—but the peculiarities of the peculiar people of God remain

There is yet a third way of understanding 'parish' and 'parochial,' this time by going back to the biblical roots. Following Ralph Neighbour, cell church writers and others concerned with process evangelism rightly call Christians to touch base with their *oikos*, their social household, their networked and meaningful relationships. But the Bible goes beyond *oikos* to talk of *paroikia*, a strange land (Acts 13.17), and *paroikos*, a resident alien (Eph 2.19, Acts 7.29). Inculturation is the necessary call of the God of mission to his church—but the peculiarities of the peculiar people of God remain.

Terry Virgo tells a story of his sister, who worked in an office and whose boss sang her praises to him—hard-working, friendly, helpful, sense of humour—and then said 'But sometimes you know, it is as if she's from another planet.'[37] The man was confronted with the paradox of a Christian life as he saw it in his own office—a citizen of his culture, but a resident alien also. 'For here we have no lasting city'—and no lasting network either—'but we are looking for that which is to come' (Hebrews 13.14).

The man was confronted with the paradox of a Christian life: a citizen of his culture, but a resident alien also

In this sense 'parish' has a cutting edge. Just as evangelism is both process and crisis, so also a mission-shaped church is both inculturated and radically counter-cultural. The integrity of the church is the lever of community and network transformation.

Some have raised questions about the tendency of the *Mission-shaped Church* report to over-emphasize inculturation. But in the end if any fresh expressions of church 'go native' and lose their distinctiveness as communities of the gospel, then they are betraying the values of the report they claim to follow. The focus of *Mission-shaped Church* is on the transformation of all life, and on the contribution of God's people to all of its flourishing.

Relational Church: Knowing and Being Known

8

> Jesus did not write a book, but formed a community.[38]
>
> Today's people...want a church made of friendship, of genuine contacts, of mutual interchange of little things. But more than anything else, a church that feeds them with the Word, a church that works with them by physically taking them by the hand, a church whose face is like that of the church of Luke, of Mark, of John, a church that is just starting—that smells of beginnings.[39]
>
> In a missionary church, a community of faith is being formed. It is characterized by welcome and hospitality. Its ethos and style are open to change when new members join.[40]

In the mid-1980s our church was using *Saints Alive,* that pioneer course in process evangelism and nurture written by John Finney and Felicity Lawson. In its first session the leaders' notes asked: 'What brings us the most happiness and the most misery? Answer—relationships!'[41]

This statement seems such a commonplace now that it is hard to remember what a bombshell it presented to many of us—certainly to me and to a church who had somehow missed this point, and was catching up only slowly with a culture which values intimacy and honesty in relationship as the touchstone of a flourishing life. In the 1970s and 1980s the battlecry of the house church movement was 'relationship, not religion.' I can clearly remember both the threat and the liberation of these words to me as an over-cerebral young vicar.

Technology is the presenting form of our culture—*The Matrix,* not *Friends*—and at first glance technology can seem the distinguishing mark of a mission-shaped church. Alt-worship, i-church. But all this makes the culture look harder-edged than it is. In fact our secular culture is a culture of intimacy.[42] Its patron saint is Diana, Princess of Wales, its favourite gadget the mobile phone, its favourite form the soap—*Friends, Coronation Street,* not *The Matrix.* (And even *The Matrix* depends in the end on interesting relationships and not on special effects—isn't that why the two sequels are not as good?).

Josephine Bax was commissioned to look at spiritual renewal across the Church of England in the mid-1980s. In her report *The Good Wine* she writes (speaking of 'renewal' in the broadest sense):

> In some of the renewed churches that I visited I experienced a quality of *koinonia* that I have previously met only in a Christian community that was living together. It was not just friendliness but the fruit of a deep commitment to Christ and to each other…the sense of the presence of God…is very attractive to many incipient Christians. They come looking to God to meet their needs and to fulfil their humanity. They stay to worship when they catch a glimpse of God at work in the body of Christ.[43]

This focus and aim has now become normative, to the point where the first common feature of fresh expressions mentioned in *Mission-shaped Church* is 'The importance of small groups for discipleship and relational mission.'[44]

The history of the church offers every generation a choice of models and methods to be considered again for now. At present Celtic spirituality is highly popular, valued for its holistic vision and spirit of respect for creation—but not only for that. In his book *The Celtic Way* Ian Bradley speaks of the transforming power of the early Celtic Christian communities which set out to be 'pools of gentleness.'[45] It is a prophetic image. Relational small groups with a shared focus on Jesus and a culture of intimacy have become the royal road to the renewal of the church in our generation. This is one key to the flavour of a mission-shaped church. The relational value carries a challenge and a critique of the inherited church, as well as looking to traditional forms for its own correction and balancing.

Technology can be used in the service of community in a relational church. This is obviously true of the internet and the increasing number of i-church experiments. But here is another application of technology:

> In an interregnum at St Leonard's, Bilston the community worker became aware of the isolation of elderly people in their homes in the parish. She set up a telephone 'link-line'; each day a volunteer would phone to ask people how they were, and whether they needed anything doing—linking with but also adding value to the social service and other provision which was poorly taken up. 'The link-line spawned a café in the rear of the church. Funding comes from the undertakers—the link-line operates as a central contact that makes arrangements for clergy to take funerals—for a fee! The local primary care trust has recognized the significance of link-line and is asking the church group if it could broaden the scheme across Wolverhampton.[46]

Electronic technology leading to café church in a postmodern society—for the over-70s! That is the relational value at work in a mission-shaped church.

Relational Leadership

Part of the thrust of *Mission-shaped Church* is to widen our expectations of the sort of people who should lead the church. For a long time we have overwhelmingly selected and trained for the pastor/teacher gifting in a Christendom church. Now this is not enough. The Ephesians 4 balance of gifts for the equipping of the saints is being revisited. Pioneer missional leaders will be gifted evangelists and gifted in the prophetic and the apostolic, and these people too need to be trained and supported and honoured.

The recommendations of the report stress the need to take this on board and to work towards it, and this is being followed up. Entrepreneurship is underrepresented in the gift mix of most of the church's leaders, and we badly need more of it. But in itself it is not the answer. In this matter too 'God looks on the heart.' *Mission-shaped Church* places a proper emphasis on training for leadership. However, as with the rest of the report, it is not just talking about ways of giving skills to people. Missionary values form missionary leaders. The notes of leadership are transparency and honesty. 'Hierarchy,' which means the rule of priests, is not a valued word in contemporary culture. And this is to the good, since neither rulers nor priests are found in leadership in the New Testament communities of faith—except that all are royal priests, and Jesus himself both Lord and high priest (see Heb 4.15, 1 Peter 2.9).

Instead of rulers and priests we see servants and friends. Jesus said 'I do not call you servants any longer…but I have called you friends.'[47]

A relational church is flexible and trusting in the way it can sit light to its own structures and favoured ways of doing things. Without trust in its leadership, no community can move fast enough to respond to its mission context. The relational value is modelled in the family of God first; 'the meeting place is the training place for the market-place.'[48]

Relational Diocese

It is in the context of the relational value that the place of the bishop in *Mission-shaped Church* needs to be weighed.[49]

Episcopal church order is relational—episcopal Christians relate to one another in communion with and in relationship with their bishop. This does not mean we have to agree with him, still less that he has to agree with us. But we define our identity within the Christian family in terms of relationship, and within the episcopal family in terms of *that* relationship. This is why the bishop is not only the broker of new ways of doing church but also the one who looks out for them, and hopefully starts them. Certainly the bishop is the one who blesses them and without whose blessing they may not thrive.

Church planting has often been resisted, although actually not often by bishops. The horror stories at the time of *Breaking New Ground* began with the resisting of church planting by territorial clergy and congregations who stood on their legal rights and were illegally (but often fruitfully) circumvented.

Mission-shaped Church comes as part of a church culture where this resisting is no longer so strong, and into a church climate where it is no longer tolerable. The review of the Pastoral Measure (which came to Synod along with *Mission-shaped Church*) will take years to bear fruit legally.[50] But the relational spirit it embodies is alive and well and leavening the church now. That spirit will abide, because it expresses a gospel value. Church planters and bishops need to relate openly and well, not because that would be good practice and good politics (although it would); but because it speaks of God whenever they do so.

9 Making Disciples: Value-based Christians

> But as for that in the good soil, these are the ones who, when they hear the word, hold it fast in an honest and good heart, and bear fruit with patient endurance.   (Luke 8.15)

We have seen that the other missionary values call the church to confidence in God, to a double listening to him and to the world, to a commitment to transform this culture and its people in the light of the kingdom, and to a focus on relationships as the key to change.

How is this to be brought about? What should we *do*?

Well, the bread is rising. Many in the church are thinking and praying about how to bring *Mission-shaped Church* off the page and onto the stage. And God is in all this. It is happening.

Already mission audits, the *Healthy Churches Handbook,* and other resources are available to help people listen and respond.

More specific resources will begin to flow soon, from the church's agencies, and from the Archbishop's 'Fresh Expressions' initiative, and from diocesan mission teams. Later, consultants will be identified—people who have tried things out, and learned the lessons of success and failure. Networks of churches will grow who can teach and learn from each other. All kinds of paths will open out before the local Christian community to make church planting and fresh expressions of church a reality in the networks and neighbourhoods where they live.

If this booklet's theme is anywhere near the truth, a mission-shaped church will begin with values and not structures

But if this booklet's theme is anywhere near the truth, a mission-shaped church will begin with values and not structures. And only local church leaders and members can lay that foundation, where the five missionary values of a mission-shaped church become the air a church breathes.

This will happen in one way only—as a result of cheerful, relentless, constant, focused, long-term repetition of these values by the church's leadership, at every opportunity, convenient or inconvenient, until people 'get them.'

So if you are in any sort of leadership in your Christian community, the fresh expression of a mission-shaped church begins here: *you repeat the importance of these values.*

Repetition, Repetition, Repetition

When you begin, your church will tell you that they sound pretty interesting. Do not be fooled. They have not got them. When you yourself start to get tired of repeating them, you can be sure that about half the people have not even heard them yet. When you are sick to death of them, then some in the church will have begun to take them on board. And when you feel like a wrung-out dishcloth from having repeated these values in sermons, in conversations, when opening the Autumn Fayre, in the Carol Service, on baptism visits, in financial reports at the AGM, at weddings, in the Deanery Synod, at the British Legion—when you feel like that, then you may be getting somewhere.

At that point people in your church may come to you and ask what the church will be doing next. They may even have read *Mission-shaped Church.* The conversation will go like this.

Them:	It's great, this *Mission-shaped Church*. I've been thinking. We could do a café church down the road!
You:	Why?
Them:	Well, the one on page 50 sounds so good. I'm sure it'll work here.
You:	Well, before we do that the incarnational value says we should listen—
Them:	Oh don't start on about that again, Vicar *(or Reader, or Pastor, or Jane, or Bill)*! Still, you may be right. Maybe it won't work after all. What about cell church instead? On page 54 there's a cracking good one…

Because they are anxious, you see. They really want to do something good for Jesus, *now*. And so do you. So at this point you take a deep breath and talk about values again, or else you will lose the plot and jump on the bandwagon. Trust me. I have the T-shirt and the bruises.

Conclusion

The foundation is our neighbour whom we must win. The neighbour is where we start. Every commandment of Christ depends on this.

Christians who are equipped with the mission-shaped heart think like this:

- **The Trinity value**—through prayer we will take the long view in God. We will be relaxed in his mission and trust in the one who has won the victory: in Jesus Christ.
- **The incarnational value**—we will listen to the people living in the networks and neighbourhoods where God has put us. And we will pray and listen to what the Lord says through his word and through one another in the church and by his Spirit. And we will do that again even after we have come up with some good ideas.
- **The transformational value**—we will look to the whole of our culture and the whole of ourselves and ask God how it can *all* be transformed through our community and our worship, to his glory.
- **The discipling value**—we will equip ourselves as God's obedient people to be salt and light and yeast in this network culture, and we will be accountable to one another and ready to lay down our preferences for the sake of the kingdom.
- **The relational value**—we will build friendships with the people

> we know, and with the bishop, and with the ones God has given us as local leaders, so that our new expression of church is 'a church that feeds them with the word, a church that works with them by physically taking them by the hand, a church whose face is like that of the church of Luke, of Mark, of John, a church that is just starting—that smells of beginnings.'

Built by Christians who live these values, church planting and fresh expressions of church will abide. And when Christians who live these values look at their context, then the mission shape of the church will drop into their imagination like ripe fruit from the tree.

And then the work of God begins...

Notes

1 A story of Abbot John the Dwarf, in Rowan Williams, *Silence and Honey Cakes*, p 25.
2 For details of that work see *Encounters on the Edge 20*, 'Soft Cell,' published by the Church Army's Sheffield Centre. Details of Sheffield Centre publications are available at www.encountersontheedge.org.uk
3 And an excellent discussion of the report is available as *Encounters on the Edge 22*, by George Lings and Bob Hopkins (Church Army, 2004).
4 Oral tradition!
5 See Ralph Neighbour, 'Where do we go from here?'; Bill Beckham, 'The Second Reformation.'
6 Rowan Williams in the *Mission-shaped Church* debate, General Synod, Feb 2004.
7 *Breaking New Ground* (Church House Publishing, 1994).
8 In *Creating Confidence in Evangelism,* the CPAS workbook for the Decade published in 1991, John Young saw this: 'The Anglican bishops world-wide in calling for a Decade of Evangelism...are more concerned with *thinking* than *doing*. They are looking for a profound change in attitude...' (p 5).
9 For instance in *Building Missionary Congregations* (Church House Publishing, 1995) and *Being Human, Being Church* (Marshall Pickering, 1995). See also his recently published *Healthy Churches Handbook* (CHP, 2004).
10 For instance in *Foolishness to the Greeks* and *The Gospel in a Pluralist Society*.
11 A phrase attributed first, I am told, to Bishop Stephen Cottrell.
12 Declaration of Assent: preface in *Common Worship* (CHP, 2000) p xi.
13 Rowan Williams, inaugural press statement as Archbishop of Canterbury-

designate, 23 July 2002.

14 'Living Proof,' *Encounters on the Edge 1* (Church Army Sheffield Centre, 1999).

15 Rowan Williams, Presidential Address to the General Synod, July 2003. For these and other statements of the Archbishop see www.archbishopof canterbury.org/sermons_speeches

16 Rowan Williams in an address to the Lambeth Partners, February 2004.

17 Rowan Williams, Presidential Address to the General Synod, July 2003.

18 *Breaking New Ground*, p vi.

19 *Mission-shaped Church*, p 81.

20 Tim Dearborn, quoted in *Mission-shaped Church*, p 85.

21 See the ACC website at www.anglicancommunion.org/mission/fivemarks.cfm

22 *Mission-shaped Church*, pp 81–2.

23 Thomas Merton, *The Wisdom of the Desert* (Sheldon Press, 1974) p 53.

24 Jesus, on many occasions (Matt 10.31, 28.10; Mk 4.40, Lk 12.32, Jn 6.20, 12.15).

25 Robert Warren, *Building Missionary Congregations*, p 20.

26 *Mission-shaped Church*, p 104.

27 Graham Cray, presenting *Mission-shaped Church* to the General Synod, Feb 2004.

28 See Ann Morisy, *Journeying Out* (Continuum Books, 2004) for a fine exposition of this thinking in the context of mission.

29 *Mission-shaped Church*, p 49. See also John Summers, *The Story of a New Way for an Anglican Parish* (New Way Publications, forthcoming).

30 Mark Greene, *Imagine* (LICC, 2003) p 11.

31 *Mission-shaped Church*, p 81.

32 Alan Ecclestone, *A Staircase for Silence* (Darton, Longman and Todd, 1977).

33 *Proceedings of the General Synod*, February 2004

34 See *Mission-shaped Church*, p 5.

35 John Stott, quoted here by Jonathan Redfearn in a sermon, see www.church.org.uk/m08dec02.htm

36 Rowan Williams, *Silence and Honey Cakes*, pp 33–34.

37 Terry Virgo, 'Building on a prophetic foundation,' taped lecture.

38 Lesslie Newbigin, *The Gospel in a Pluralist Society*, p 223.

39 Carlo Carretto, *I sought and I found*, p 34.

40 *Mission-shaped Church*, p 82.

41 *Saints Alive!* by John Finney and Felicity Lawson (ARM, 1982) p 17.

42 See Theodore Zeldin, 'A culture of intimacy' *Observer* newspaper article, September 1997 (the week of Princess Diana's death). Also the same writer's *An Intimate History of Humanity* (1994)

43 Josephine Bax, *The Good Wine*, pp 13-14.

44 *Mission-shaped Church*, p 43.

45 Ian Bradley, *The Celtic Way* (DLT, 1993).

46 I am grateful to Ann Morisy for telling me the story of Bilston.

47 John 10.14, 15.15. See also Paul Bayes 'To Know and Be Known: friendship as a paradigm for ministry in the church' (available from paul.bayes@c-of-e.org.uk).

48 A phrase of John Wimber, often used by Bishop David Pytches. See, for example, *Come Holy Spirit* (Hodder and Stoughton, 1986).

49 See the chapter 'An Enabling Framework' in *Mission-shaped Church*, pp 125ff.

50 'A Measure for Measures,' General Synod paper.